LIFE IN FREEDOM

and

The Dissolution of the Order of the Star

by

J. Krishnamurti

THE BOOK TREE
San Diego, California

Life in Freedom
copyright 1928
Horace Liveright
New York

The Dissolution of the Order of the Star
A Statement by J. Krishnamurti
copyright 1929
The Star Publishing Trust
Eerde, Ommen, Holland

additional material and revisions
© 2016
The Book Tree
All rights reserved

ISBN 978-1-58509-371-7

Cover Image
© Gts

Cover Layout
Mike Sparrow

Published by
The Book Tree
P O Box 16476
San Diego, CA 92176
www.thebooktree.com

We provide fascinating and educational products to help awaken the public to new ideas and information that would not be available otherwise.
Call 1 (800) 700-8733 for our *FREE BOOK TREE CATALOG*.

THIS book has been compiled by the Author from Camp-Fire addresses given in Benares, Ojai and Ommen during 1928.

CONTENTS

	PAGE
THE PURPOSE OF LIFE	9
HAPPINESS AND DESIRE	17
UNDERSTANDING	31
THE SEARCH	47
STAND IN YOUR OWN STRENGTH	67
THE HIDDEN WELL	73
BE IN LOVE WITH LIFE	77
TIME	83
FORMLESS CREATION	89

INTRODUCTION

Jiddu Krishnamurti was one of the greatest spiritual teachers of modern times. While very young he was seen as something special so he and his brother were adopted by Annie Besant of the Theosophical Society and brought to England in 1911. He was groomed to be the next World Teacher, which Theosophists had been predicting would come. A worldwide organization was created around him called The Order of the Star of the East, which became enormously popular. In 1927 he was officially recognized by the group as being the World Teacher, but was not comfortable in this role. He was a man of great wisdom by this time-one whose ego did not need validation from this role; nor did he believe that he could "save" others, as was often being asked of him.

This book is a collection of talks from 1928. They impart useful wisdom to the listener/reader, rather than create a dependency on him. These talks often contradict the expectations of him, and instead provide the reader with tools to live a "Life In Freedom." It was something he sought as well. In 1929, shortly after this book came out, Krishnamurti renounced his role and dissolved The Order of the Star. He returned all the property and money that had come with his position and left with nothing-except Freedom. A rare, 14-page announcement, The Dissolution of the Order of the Star, was distributed to his followers. It is included here as an addendum, which allows this book to be seen in a better context.

Krishnamurti was in fact a great world teacher who, to many, turned out better than what was expected of him. He cast his ego aside and taught people how to empower themselves. He understood the inner strength we have available and how one can access it-without depending on groups or outside agencies that might claim to provide one with salvation. In a quieter and more powerful way, he continued teaching up to his death in 1986. This book outlines the main ideas of his life's work, which caused his break with the Order of the Star. These ideas were so powerful they could not be denied. Chapters include The Purpose of Life, Happiness and Desire, Understanding, The Search, Stand In Your Own Strength, The Hidden Well, Be in Love With Life, Time, and Formless Creation.

Paul Tice

THE PURPOSE OF LIFE

AS the shadows were awakening and a scent of the morn was carried on the breeze, I saw an eagle descending from the mountain-tops. It came down without a flutter of the wings into the valley, and there disappeared among the shadows of the black mountains. At the end of the day I saw it return again to its abode among the mountain peaks, far away from the strife, the struggle and the jostle of the world.

So is the man who has seen the vision of the Truth, who has during his strife in the world, established for himself the eternal goal. Though he may wander among the transient things, and lose himself among the shadows, yet all his life will be guided by that goal. As the eagle soars to its abode, so will he soar beyond all sorrows, beyond all fleeting pleasures and passing joys.

The establishment of that eternal goal is of primary importance for one who desires to disentangle himself from all the complications of life—not the goal of another, nor the vision of another, but the goal that is born of his own experience, his own sorrow, suffering, and understanding. Such a goal, when once it is established, will throw light on the confusion of all thought, and thereby make clear the purpose of life.

As a ship that is lost at sea without a compass, so the man without the perception of the goal which is constant and eternal, is lost in this world of confusion. As the captain of a ship establishes the destination of his vessel and by the compass is able to guide his course through stormy nights and dark waters, so the man who has knowledge of his goal can guide his life by that compass of understanding.

Because the individual does not know his purpose, he is in a state of uncertainty and chaos. Because the individual has not solved his own problem, the problem of the world has not been solved. The individual problem is the world problem. If an individual is unhappy, discontented, dissatisfied, then the world around him is in sorrow, discontent and ignorance. If the individual has not found his goal, the world will not find its goal. You cannot separate the individual from the world. The world and the individual are one. If the individual problem

THE PURPOSE OF LIFE

can be solved by understanding, so can the problem of the world be solved. Before you can give understanding to others you have first to understand for yourself. When you establish the Truth in your heart and mind, there it will abide eternally.

One day in Benares I was going in a boat down the sacred Ganges, watching the people on the river banks worshiping God in search of happiness, in search of their goal and the way of its attainment. I saw one man in deep meditation, forgetting everything around him, holding but the one thought in his mind—to find and to attain the goal. I saw another performing rites required by his system of yoga. I saw another repeating chants, lost to the world and to himself. They were all seeking what you are seeking, what every one in the world is seeking in moments of deep thought, and of great desire.

As the boat is carried down the stream by the current, so is every one carried away by his desires, by his passions and longings, because not one has found or established his purpose. Because the goal has not been established, because the path that leads to that goal has not been found, there is confusion and chaos, there is questioning and doubt in the mind. As long as there is doubt in the mind there is no peace, nor certainty and ecstasy of purpose.

This condition exists throughout the world, but everywhere there is a heart beating and a mind capable of thought. Man everywhere is unconsciously seeking a way to free himself from his narrowness, his pettiness. The end of this search is freedom and eternal happiness. He experiments along many paths, and every path leads to complications. From life to life he wanders, from shrine to shrine, from one creed to another—gathering experience, accepting, rejecting, and again accepting—thus he goes forward towards that goal which awaits him as it awaits all men.

In the process of accumulation and rejection, he does not know which way to turn for comfort, and when he seeks comfort through any particular channel he is enmeshed and entangled. Because there are many interpreters of the Truth, because there are many conflicting paths, beliefs and religions, man is lost in their complexities. As a butterfly that knocks against the windowpane, struggling to escape into the fresh air and the open sky, so do men struggle when they have not caught a glimpse

THE PURPOSE OF LIFE

of the goal—but it is not hard to establish. It is because they are in darkness that the goal seems far away.

As the potter molds the clay to the delight of his imagination, so can man mold his life through the desire of his heart. As the earthen vessels are fashioned into beautiful or ugly forms, so life can be made beautiful or ugly according to the purpose which you have established for yourself.

I would help you to that goal which you are seeking, which you desire to attain—the goal which awaits all the peoples of the world, whatever their experiences, thoughts or feelings. Then you will be able to guide yourself through the darkness of the world as a man guides himself of a dark night by the stars.

If you once establish such a goal—which is happiness and hence freedom—life becomes simple. There is no longer confusion, and time, and the complications of time, disappear. It is because you have not established your goal that the present is as the mountain when the sun has set—the light fails and the darkness of the mountain overshadows the valley. Time is only

LIFE IN FREEDOM

a binder of life and the moment you are free you are beyond time. Then you can guide yourself without depending upon any authority. Then you will no longer have fear. Then for you there will be no conflict of good and evil. When you have set life free you will find happiness, which is the only goal, the only absolute Truth.

HAPPINESS AND DESIRE

HAPPINESS AND DESIRE

BECAUSE man has forgotten that the true purpose of his being is to cultivate happiness within himself and in those around him, there is confusion and chaos, and his actions but add to that chaos.

What is it for which every one in the world is craving and longing? To find happiness. True happiness is neither selfish, nor negative. It is intelligence, the accumulation of all experience; it is Truth which is eternal. No cloud can hide it nor can any sorrow lessen it. It is such happiness that every one desires. It is such happiness that I have always desired. I have seen people weighed down with labor, performing great works, accumulating knowledge, struggling to be spiritual and yet they had forgotten the one thing—happiness—which alone gives life to the mind and nourishment to the heart. There can be no health except in happiness. He who has not found it will never find Truth, will never bring life to its fulfillment, will never have tranquillity in this world of travail.

If you desire to establish that happiness within yourself, you must make it your goal and then your life will be as the flame which soars heavenwards.

People in search of happiness resort to many things—they will worship at temples and churches, they will gather from books the knowledge of others, they will perform religious rites in the hope of establishing in their minds peace and tranquillity. The desire for happiness is ever gnawing at their hearts.

In the great continent of America they are making the physical predominant in search for happiness. They say that without physical comfort, without a body that is strong and healthy, there cannot be a right development of the emotions. But in trying to establish perfect physical conditions they are losing sight of other essential things. In India, they go to the opposite extreme and in search for happiness they neglect altogether the physical.

Look where you will, every human being is seeking happiness. He begins his search in the mere pleasures which come from physical excitement. Then discovering that this excite-

HAPPINESS AND DESIRE

ment does not satisfy his craving for the lasting happiness, he experiments with other experiences, mental and emotional.

Life is a process of accumulating and discarding, of gathering and setting aside. What you gather you reject, and the more you reject the nearer you are to liberation. By setting aside what you have gained, you acquire the knowledge which will give you strength to shape your purpose, which will give you power ultimately to reach the Kingdom of Happiness which each one of you seeks.

As there is sap in the tree which brings forth foliage for the glory of its being, so in each man there is the spark of divinity which through sorrow, through ecstasy, through struggle, through all the processes of life, grows to perfection, to that state of eternal happiness which is the goal for all, which is the truest spirituality —the greatest gift that any one can give to another.

You will find this undying, unalterable happiness when you are liberated from the tyrannies of the self—its desires and longings. This is not a goal imposed upon you by another. It is the longing of every human soul, of every individual who is striving, who is in sorrow, who is seeking. It is the spark of this desire which grows into a flame and becomes part of the Eternal Flame, and when you are able to lose yourself in that Flame, then you are in the Kingdom of Happiness.

Each must discover his own way of attainment. There is no other truth or other god but that goal which each one has established for himself, which cannot be destroyed by the breath of man or by the passing whims of any god.
In what way can you attain this goal and hold this happiness eternally in your heart? If you are a thoughtful person, you will recognize that in every one there are three different beings—the mind, the emotions and the body. And if you observe you will find that each of these beings has a separate existence of its own and tries to create and to act independently of the others, thus causing disharmony. Absolute happiness comes from the establishment of harmony between these three. If you are driving three horses—each desiring to run independently of the other two—unless you are able to con-

HAPPINESS AND DESIRE

trol them and drive them all together, you will not reach your destination.

The mind must have a goal of its own, but it must be a goal created by you yourself; otherwise it will lead to superstition.

What is the ultimate goal for the mind?

It is the purification of the self, which means the development of individual uniqueness.

As the seed is forced by the life within it to break through the heavy earth and come into light, so if you are urged by the desire to find freedom, you will break through all limitations which bind you. To gain freedom, great desire is needed. People are afraid of desire, thinking that it is something evil which must be destroyed. But this is a mistaken attitude. Desire is the motive power behind all action. If you would light a great fire to warm and comfort you, you must give fuel to it, feed it with great logs of wood. So if you would fulfill life you must have great desires, for desire brings experience and experience leads to knowledge. If a man knows how to use desire it will bring him to the freedom for which he longs. If desire is killed or suppressed, there is no possibility of freedom. Most people in the world have intense, burning, vital desires but instead of utilizing them and training them, they either suppress them or are controlled by them. Without desire there can be no creative work. If you kill desire you become like a piece of dead wood, or else you become an automaton, a machine. Machines have been invented to minimize human labor. Physical problems perhaps may be solved in this way, but mental and emotional problems are more difficult to solve, and because the way to solve these problems is so little understood, religions, creeds, and dogmas have been invented.

If desire gives life it should be encouraged. If desire creates sorrow, through understanding that sorrow must be overcome. Because man does not want to be free, he kills his desires; because he does not want to attain true liberation, he is making of himself a machine. Use desire as a stepping-stone to kindle greater desires, to awaken greater delight and longing.

But intelligence is necessary in order to develop your individual uniqueness, to purify your desires, to realize that self which is the self of all—to realize that absolute union with all things which brings to an end the sense of separation. It is necessary for the mind to be simple,

HAPPINESS AND DESIRE

but simplicity does not mean crudeness. We should not turn our back upon the results of progress and evolution, but on the contrary we should utilize them. A mind that is simple will understand perfection because it is part of perfection itself. A mind that is crooked cannot understand the Truth. A mind that is complicated, that is full of the knowledge of books—though they have their value—is apt to become crystallized. In all great architecture, painting and sculpture, in all the greatest forms of beauty, there is simplicity and there is restraint. Simplicity of the mind is the greatest and most difficult thing to acquire, but in order to be simple you must have had great experience. Simplicity of the truest kind is the highest form of spirituality.

What is the ultimate goal for the emotions? It is affectionate detachment. To be able to love and yet not be attached to any one or anything is the absolute perfection of emotion.

As a barren tree in winter without leaf or flower to give scent to the morning air, so is a man without love. Those who would attain to Truth must cultivate—as the gardener cultivates his garden—this flower of affection, which is to give delight, which is to be a source of comfort in disappointment and sorrow. Love—however envious, jealous, tyrannical, selfish it may be at first—is a bud that will grow into great glory and give the scent of its perfection to every passer-by. Without love man is as a desert of dry sand, as the river in the summer time, without water to nourish its banks. Those who would attain the perfection of happiness, the beauty that is hidden from the human eye, must cultivate this quality of love. You must love all and yet be detached from all, for love is necessary to the unfoldment of life. To cultivate it you must learn to observe, you must gather experience—vicariously, or through your own treading of the sorrowful paths of experience. It is through experience that you know sympathy, that you are able to give affection to those who desire it, for if you have never experienced sorrow then your heart is incapable of sympathy and understanding.

This does not mean that you should taste of everything. There are many ways of acquiring experience—one is by living in the life of every one, looking through the eyes of every passer-by and experiencing in imagination his sorrow, his transient pleasures. When you see a drunken

HAPPINESS AND DESIRE

man in the street, it should be sufficient to give you the experience of drunkenness; if you see a man in tears, that should give you the experience of grief; if you see a man in joy and ecstasy, that should give you the experience of joy. We need not all follow one road of knowledge. We give and take from each other. We can gather knowledge from the experience of the whole world and that is sufficient for progress, for culture and refinement. If you would attain to the fulfillment of life, you must have this accumulation of experience, for without experience you cannot arrive at the goal, you cannot unite the beginning and the end. While there is separation, there is pain, and it is only in the union with the goal that there is happiness, that you establish lasting Truth within yourself. To do that, you must from the very beginning gather experience as a man gathers the grain of the field.

If you have no sympathy, no affection, you can never achieve, you can never identify yourself with the goal. A mind that is contented and satisfied will never acquire sympathy or affection or give understanding to others. I have watched people who have greatly desired to help others but they do not know how to help.

They are incapable of putting themselves into the place of another and so envisaging his point of view.

Those who would understand the life around them, who would see the goal and thereby establish the Beloved in their hearts, must develop great love and yet be detached from the bondage of that love. They must have great sympathy and yet not be bound by that sympathy. They must have great desires and yet not be slaves of those desires.

What is the ultimate goal for the body?

Every one in the world is seeking for beauty but they seek without understanding. It is essential for the body to be beautiful, but it must not be a mere shell of beauty without beautiful thought and feeling. Restraint is necessary for the body—control without suppression.

These are the essentials for the absolute harmony of the three beings in each of us.

The desire for freedom, the desire to escape from all things, or rather to transcend all things, is necessary for the attainment of perfection. You can only free yourself if your mind and

HAPPINESS AND DESIRE

heart have determined their purpose in life and are continually struggling towards it, never yielding to those things which create barriers between yourself and your goal.

To attain perfection, to walk towards the goal of Truth which is eternal happiness for all, at whatever stage of evolution you may be, it is necessary to be rid of the binding narrow traditions that are born out of blind belief and have no touch with life.

As when the rains come, only those who have prepared their fields and removed the weeds will have the full produce of their labor, the full benefit of the rain, so, if you would have the Beloved always with you, you must remove from your mind and heart the complicated ideas, traditions, and narrow points of view, which are as weeds that kill true understanding. For without understanding there can be no coöperation with life.

UNDERSTANDING

UNDERSTANDING

For the well-being of the mind and heart, understanding is as essential as a warm fire on a cold night.

People imagine that they can attain by some miraculous process, that they can find Truth by the mere outward form of worship, that they can discover their goal by the continual repetition of prayers and chants, or by the performance of yoga, puja and other rites. You can only discover that which you desire, that for which your heart longs, and for which your mind craves, by yourself, through the purification of the heart and mind.

If you would understand Truth you must remove from your heart those stones and weeds which strangle its full growth.

Where there is narrowness of mind and limitation of heart, Truth cannot enter. If you would climb to that height where there are eternal snows, you must leave behind you the accumulation of your possessions, you must be hardened and well trained; and your heart must be filled with the desire of attainment.

For those who have no fixed purpose there is renunciation and self-sacrifice; there is sorrow, grief and pain, endless struggle and violent dissatisfaction. But for those who have the fixed purpose to attain the Truth which is the unfoldment of life—though they may dwell in the valley of the shadows—there is no sacrifice, there is no struggle.

Because you have no fixed purpose all the shadows of the valley entice you, wrap you in their soft fogs, so that you lose the ecstasy of life. But if you have established your goal, which is the goal of the world—the attainment of the Kingdom of Happiness through freedom from all experience—then you can control the future, then you are the creator of that which you desire. If you can pass through the valley of the shadows with eyes eternally fixed upon the mountain-top, then you can have all experiences without creating barriers between yourself and the goal. This is the understanding of life which will bring order out of chaos and it is for that purpose that the Beloved has come. As the true artist, who by his imagina-

UNDERSTANDING

tion creates beauty out of the chaos around him, out of the confusion which exists in the world, so the Beloved, Truth, creates order in the mind and heart of those who understand. When you understand, you will have solved the problem of your daily life. If there is no struggle within to free yourself from the cage of sorrow and pain, from the limitations which cause confusion, then, however much I may knock at the door of your heart, there will be no response. But the moment you yourself are dissatisfied, the moment you yourself desire to escape and to attain liberation, then you yourself seek the source of Truth.

Those who seek for an understanding of life, must fix their inward perception on eternal Truth which is the unfolding of life.

To those who live and have their being in the valley, the mountains are mysterious, hard, cruel, eternally aloof. The mountains never change; they are ever constant, never yielding. So it is with Truth. To those who live in the valley of shadows, of transient things, Truth seems terrible, hard and cruel.

Everywhere, among all people, there is a

search for something hidden, for some realization which will give wisdom, greater knowledge, greater vision, greater understanding; this the people call Truth.

They think that Truth lies hidden in some distant place, away from life, away from joy, away from sorrow. But Truth is life, and with an understanding of life there is born an understanding of Truth. When you are fulfilling life with understanding you are the master of Truth.

Though there is at the present time a revolt against tradition and the established order of things, against morality in the narrow sense, yet the majority of people still judge and try to understand life from the prejudiced point of view of a limited and settled mind. A Hindu will only recognize Truth when it is presented to him through the medium of Hinduism, and so it is with the Christian and the Buddhist. But Truth is never contained in a particular form or medium. Truth can only be understood with an unbiased mind, capable of detachment and pure judgment.

As every human being is divine, so every individual in the world should be his own master, his own absolute ruler and guide. But if he

UNDERSTANDING

would guide himself intelligently, he must be able to judge all things with an open mind and not reject what he does not understand because he is prejudiced.

Truth is the power within each one of you which urges you on to attainment. It is the consummation of all intelligence. It is Absolute. There is no god except the man who has purified himself and so has attained to Truth.

When you bind life to beliefs and traditions, to codes of morality, you kill life. In order to keep alive, vital, ever changing, ever growing, as the tree that is ever putting out new leaves, you must give to life the opportunities, the nourishment which will strengthen it and make it grow. When life desires to find its freedom the only way by which it can attain is through experience.

There can be no understanding of life, which is Truth, when there is not the thrill, the agony, the suffering, the continual upheaval, discouragement and encouragement of life.

In the olden days, especially in India, those who desired to find Truth imagined that they could discover the way by withdrawing from the aching world, from the transient things, from the shadow of the real, by the destruction of the physical. But now you have to face life as it is, for you can only conquer life, when you have a complete and not a partial understanding of it.

Once there was a man who kept all the windows of his house well closed except one, hoping that through that window alone the sun-light would come, but it never came. That is what those people are doing who are bound by tradition, by narrow sectarian beliefs, and who think that Truth is contained in any of those beliefs. You cannot bind life, which is the Truth, by anything, for life must be free and untrammeled. If you do not understand that the purpose of life is freedom, then you are only gilding the bars of your cage by the invention of theories, of creeds, of philosophies and religions.

The basis of all these innumerable beliefs is fear. You are afraid for your salvation, you are afraid to test your own knowledge, and hence you rely on the assertions, on the authority of another.

In order to be happy need we have religions? In order to love need we build temples? In or-

UNDERSTANDING

der to fulfill the self need we worship a personal god?

You must give to the suffering world, not beliefs, creeds, dogmas, but new understanding which comes from intelligent coöperation with Nature, through observation of all the events of daily life.

Those who would understand Truth, who would give of their heart and their mind to that Truth, must first have grown in experience. Then experience will guide them, for experience gives intelligence, and intelligence is the accumulation of all experience. The web of life is spun out of common things and the common things are experience.

Learn from every event, from every activity in daily life, and assimilate the experience every moment of the day.

You go to temples or to churches or to other places of worship and there you imagine that you are purified. But does that purification stand the test of daily life?

Your theories, your superficial knowledge of life, do not help you at moments of crisis. When death comes and takes away your friend, your beliefs and theories do not help you to overcome your loneliness and the sense of separation. You will only overcome it if the poison of separation has been destroyed, and you can only destroy that sense of separation by observing others in sorrow, in pain and in pleasure like yourself, and finding that in suffering as well as in pleasure there is unity.

No one can develop that power which dwells within you but yourself, for that power grows by experience. But experience alone, undirected by the goal you would attain, produces chaos, the chaos which prevails in the world at present. Without the understanding of the purpose of life there is bound to be chaos.

The first demand upon those who would seek the understanding of true happiness, is that they should have the burning longing to be free from all things, to gain that freedom which comes when you are beyond the need for further experience because you have passed through all experience.

If you would understand what I mean by the freedom of life, you must establish for yourself the goal which is liberation even from life itself.

For the understanding of life you must have revolt, dissatisfaction and great discontentment.

UNDERSTANDING

Many people in the world imagine that they have found Truth by adopting some theory or other, and hence that they have solved the whole problem of life.

Contentment without understanding is like a pool covered with green scum, which does not reflect the bare eye of heaven. It is very easy to be ignorantly discontented, but to be discontented and to revolt intelligently is a divine gift. Revolt with intelligence, with understanding, is as a great river that is full of power.

Revolt is essential in order to escape from the narrowness of tradition, from the binding influences of belief, of theories. If you would understand the Truth, you must be in revolt so that you may escape from all these—from books, from theories, from gods, from superstitions —from everything which is not of your own.

If you would understand the meaning of my words, then throw aside all your mental conceptions of life and begin again from the very beginning. Then you will see for yourself how life works, how life which is the accumulation of all experience speaks through that voice which we call intuition, which guides you and helps you on the onward path.

LIFE IN FREEDOM

I would urge you to be free—free from the very gods whom you worship, from the very beings whom you hold dear, because freedom is necessary for the growth of the soul and without freedom there is decay.

Because you do not wish to be free, you seek comfort, and comfort is like the shadow of a tree, it varies according to the sun from moment to moment, and those who seek comfort must move from one abode to another. Comfort cannot dwell with understanding.

The man who seeks comfort, who searches for the satisfaction of the moment, will never find real and lasting joy, for the momentary comfort is as transitory as the flower that is born of a morning and withers at the ending of the day.

When a pond is not touched with the breath of air, the waters become stagnant, and no animal comes to it to slake its thirst. But when the fresh winds come and breathe on its face, then animals and human beings alike can quench their thirst.

So if there is not in you the fresh wind of desire for freedom from all things, you will not find the Truth which alone can remove the thirst of the world.

UNDERSTANDING

When you are free, as the bird in the skies, your life becomes simple. Life is complicated only when there is limitation. Then you need traditions and beliefs to uphold you.

But when you desire to be free from all things, then you break away from the old order and enter upon that new life which will lead you towards perfection which is liberation and happiness.

When you are able to become a flame of revolt, then the means to reach the Kingdom will be found.

We have to create a miracle of order in this century of chaos and superstition. But first we have to create order in ourselves, a lasting order which is not based on fear or on authority.

I have found and established for myself that which is eternal, and it is my work to create order in your mind, so that you will no longer depend on outward authority, no longer be the slave of superstition or of those trivialities which hold life in bondage, and divide you from your goal.

Because you have no true purpose in life there is chaos within you; there is misery without understanding, strife without purpose, struggle in ignorance. But when you have established the goal of the Beloved in your heart and mind there is understanding in your life. There may still be struggle but it will be with understanding, and there will be greater love and greater happiness. Establish, therefore, within you that which is eternal, and the present shadows will pass away.

When you have established the Beloved in your heart, the source and the end are united and time no longer exists, for you hold eternity within you.

When you have established the Beloved in your heart, you are ready to face the open seas, where there are great storms, and the strong breezes which quicken life.

Because you have the Beloved in your heart, you must be a lighthouse on a dark shore, to guide those who are still enshrouded in their own darkness.

Of what value is your understanding, of what value are your high and noble thoughts, your pure life, if you do not help those who are in constant pain, who are in darkness, and in confusion? Of what value is the Truth you have seen if you are not able to give of that Truth to

UNDERSTANDING those who are hungering and thirsting after the eternal?

Because you have understood, be courageous with that understanding, and give of your life to those who are in darkness.

THE SEARCH

THE SEARCH

IF you would see life as a clear picture you must, by discriminating and selecting from your many experiences, gather the knowledge which will help you to the attainment of your goal. Life cannot be separated from thought, feeling and action, and when you understand life as a whole, using all experience as a ladder on which to climb, you attain.

My purpose is to make clear to you your own desires, to strengthen your own unique growth towards perfection. But if you merely obey me or use me as an authority, as a stepping-stone towards your goal, you will fail, because it will not be your own desire that urges you. Whereas, if you strengthen the understanding of your own desire and use all experience to that end, no one can destroy or take away that which you have gained.

As from out of a fire there comes forth a spark which can in its turn light a great flame, springing heavenwards, so in every man there is born the spark of desire, and I would strengthen that desire in you that you may be able for yourself to light the fire which is necessary for the fulfillment of life.

To follow another, whosoever he may be, is to me the very negation of what I hold to be true. Worship is contrary to all my ideas, especially worship of individuals, and if you regard me as an authority when this form of mine passes away you will again be bound to the same wheel of limitation. I do not want followers, I do not want disciples, I do not want praise or worship of any kind. I need nothing from any one.

The time when one left the world and went away to a secluded spot, to a monastery, is past. The time for open life and clear understanding has come and I would speak of that understanding which I have found. I would show you how I have found my Beloved, how the Beloved is established in me, how the Beloved is the Beloved of all and how the Beloved and I are one so that there can be no separation either now or at any time.

I have long been in revolt from all things, from the authority of others, from the instruction of others, from the knowledge of others; I would not accept anything as Truth until I found the Truth myself. I never opposed the ideas of others but I would not accept their authority, their theory of life. Until I was in that state of revolt, until I became dissatisfied with everything, with every creed, with every dogma and belief, I was not able to find the Truth. Until I was able to destroy these things by constant struggle to understand what lies behind them, I was not able to attain the Truth I sought. Naturally, I did not think of all these things while I was young. They grew in me unconsciously but now I can place all the events of my life in their proper order and see in what manner I have developed to attain my goal, and have become my goal.

For long I have searched for that goal, and during my search I have watched people trapped in their desires, as a fly is caught in the web of a spider. Ever since I was able to think I have watched people absorbed in their own thoughts, suffocated by the futility of life. Wherever I went I saw people who believed that their happiness consisted in the multitude of possessions. I saw people who had all the comforts of this world, and yet their lives were in confusion because they were enslaved by these things. I saw

LIFE IN FREEDOM

people who loved greatly and yet were bound by their love, for they had not found the way to give love and yet be free. I saw people who were wise in knowledge; and yet they were bound by their very learning. I saw people who were steeped in religion and yet they were bound by their traditions and by their fear of the unknown.

I saw the wise withdraw from the world into their own seclusion, and the ignorant caught up in their own labors.

Watching people thus I have seen that they build for themselves walls of prejudice, walls of belief, walls of credulous thought, walls of great fear against which they fight, trying to escape from the very walls they themselves have built. Watching all people I have seen how useless is their struggle if they are not free from the very gods they worship, from the interpreters who would guide them. Each guide, each interpreter of the Truth translates that Truth according to his own limited vision. If you depend on the interpreter for your understanding you will only learn the Truth according to his limitations. But if you establish the goal for yourself, if you strengthen your own desire for Truth and test the keenness of that desire by observation, by

THE SEARCH

welcoming sorrow and experience, then you need have no mediators, then there need exist nothing between you and your goal, between you and the Truth.

I would that I could make you certain of the Truth, for Truth is greater than every book of every religion, greater than every belief that you hold dear. But because you do not understand, Truth appears to you as something fearsome, an enemy to be conquered, and because of this fear you seek a mediator. But if you have a pure heart and a mind that is full with understanding, you do not need *gurus*, mediators who must inevitably condition, limit, the Truth.

Ever since I was young I have observed these things and I have never allowed myself to be caught up in any of these confusions. Because I have established my goal, because I have always regarded myself as a boat on the stream, having no connection with the land, where there is confusion, I have attained, and now I would share my experience with others. I would help those who are confused to make their minds and hearts simple in their desire for attainment.

Ever since I was a boy I have been, as most young people are, or should be, in revolt. Nothing satisfied me. I listened, I observed, I wanted something beyond mere phrases, the *maya* of words. I wanted to discover and to establish for myself a goal. I did not want to rely on any one. I do not remember the time when I was being molded in my boyhood! but I can look back and see how nothing satisfied me.

When I went to Europe for the first time I lived among people who were wealthy and well educated, who held positions of social authority; but whatever their dignities or distinctions, they could not satisfy me. I was in revolt also against theosophists with all their jargon, their theories, their meetings, and their explanations of life. When I went to a meeting, the lecturers repeated the same ideas which did not satisfy me or make me happy. I went to fewer and fewer meetings, I saw less and less of the people who merely repeated the ideas of Theosophy. I questioned everything because I wanted to find out for myself.

I walked about the streets, watching the faces of people who perhaps watched me with even greater interest. I went to theaters, I saw how people amused themselves trying to forget their unhappiness, thinking that they were solving their problems by drugging their hearts and minds with superficial excitement.

THE SEARCH

I saw people with political, social or religious power—and yet they did not have that one essential thing in their lives, which is happiness.

I attended labor meetings, communist meetings, and listened to what their leaders had to say. They were generally protesting against something. I was interested but they did not give me satisfaction.

By observation of one type and another I gathered experience vicariously. Within every one there was a latent volcano of unhappiness and discontent. I passed from one pleasure to another, from one amusement to another, in search of happiness and found it not. I watched the amusements of the young people, their dances, their dresses, their extravagances, and I saw that they were not happy with the happiness which I was seeking. I watched people who had very little in life, who wanted to tear down those things which others had built up. They thought that they were solving life by destroying and building differently and yet they were unhappy.

I saw people who desired to serve going into those quarters where the poor and the degraded live. They desired to help but were themselves helpless. How can you cure another of disease if you are yourself a victim of that disease?

I saw people satisfied with the stagnation which is unproductive, uncreative—the bourgeois type which never struggles to be above the surface or falls below it and so feels its weight.

I read books on philosophy, on religion, biographies of great people and yet they could not give me what I wanted. I wanted to be so certain, so positive, in my attitude towards life that nothing could disturb me.

Then I came to India and I saw that the people there were deluding themselves equally, carrying on the same old traditions, treating women cruelly. At the same time they called themselves very religious and painted their faces with ashes. In India they may have the most sacred books in the world, they may have the greatest philosophies, they may have constructed wonderful temples in the past, but none of these was able to give me what I wanted. Neither in Europe nor in India could I find happiness.

Still I wandered always in search of this happiness which I knew must exist. This was not a merely intellectual or emotional conviction. It was like the hidden perfection, which cannot

THE SEARCH

be described, but of whose existence you are certain. You cannot ask a bud how it opens, in what manner it gives forth its scent, at what time of the morning it unfolds itself to the sun. But if you watch carefully, if you observe keenly, you will discover for yourself the hidden beauty of perfection.

Still lacking the fixed purpose from which comes the delight of living, I went to California. Circumstances forced me there because my brother was ill. There among the hills we lived in a small house in complete retirement, doing everything for ourselves. If you would discover Truth you must for a time withdraw from the world. In that retired spot my brother and I talked much together. We meditated, trying to understand, for meditation of the heart is understanding.

There I was naturally driven within myself and I learned that as long as I had no definite goal or purpose in life, I was, like the rest of mankind, tossed about as a ship on a stormy sea. With that in my mind, after rejecting all lesser things, I established for myself my goal. I wanted to enter into eternal happiness. I wanted to become the very goal. I wanted to drink from the source of life. I wanted to unite the beginning and the end. I fixed that goal as my Beloved and that Beloved is Life, the Life of all things. I wanted to destroy the separation that exists between man and his goal. I said to myself that as long as there is this void of separation between myself and my goal there is bound to be misery, disturbance and doubt. There will be authority which I must obey, to which I must yield. As long as there is separation between you and me there is unhappiness for us both. So I set about destroying all the barriers that I had previously erected. I began to reject, to renounce, to set aside what I had gathered and little by little I approached my goal.

When my brother died, the experience it brought me was great, not the sorrow—sorrow is momentary and passes away, but the joy of experience remains. If you understand life rightly then death becomes an experience out of which you can build your house of perfection, your house of delight. When my brother died, that gap of separation still existed in me; I saw him once or twice after death but that did not satisfy me. How can you be satisfied alone? You may invent phrases, you may have great

THE SEARCH

knowledge of books; but as long as there is within you separation and loneliness, there is sorrow. Because I desired to establish life within myself, because I desired to become united with the goal, I struggled. Life is a process of struggle, of continuous gathering of the dust of experience.

If you are lost on a dark night and you see a distant light, you make your way towards that light with bleeding feet, through bogs, through pitfalls, through difficulties, because you know that the light indicates a human dwelling. So have I walked and struggled towards that light which is my goal, which is the goal of all humanity because it is humanity itself. All the pitfalls, all the things which entangle, all the things which hurt, are transient and pass away. I suffered but I set about to free myself from everything that bound me, till in the end I became united with the Beloved, I entered into the sea of liberation and established that liberation within me.

The simple union with the Beloved, the direct way of attainment, which is the eternal way, gives ecstasy to life. If you search for Truth in the realms of *maya*, in the realm of the intellect or of mere emotionalism, or in the physical sense-world alone, you will never find it. Yet when you have found it you realize that it is contained in them all. You cannot separate life from any expression of life and yet you must be able to distinguish between life and its expressions. Because at first I tried to separate life from the goal, because to me life was one thing and knowledge another, everything became confused and I turned for support to tradition, to comfort, to self-contentment and satisfaction. When you perceive the light of your goal you are guided by it as a ship is guided by a lighthouse on a dark shore. When you have seen that vision of perfection, that hidden beauty which cannot be explained in words, which is beyond intellectual theories and mere emotional excitement, it will act as your eternal guide, it will shed its light upon your path and whatever your experience or lack of experience may be, you will attain. Attainment is not for the few but for all, at whatever stage of evolution they may be. You can perceive the Beloved when you have learned to translate the ordinary sorrows and pleasures of life into terms

THE SEARCH

of eternal Truth. If you can interpret all experience in the light of your goal, then you will become united with that goal.

Because I am united eternally, inseparably with my Beloved—who is the Beloved of all, who is yourself—I would show you the way, because you are in pain, in sorrow, in doubt. But I can only be a sign-post for you. You must have the strength of your own desire to attain. You must experience the pain and the sorrow in your own self. You must strive for yourself. Your desire must come from your very soul. It must be the result of your own experience, for by that alone will you attain.

By telling you of my attainment I do not wish to create authority because if I create authority in your mind I shall destroy your own perception of the Truth. I want to make you breathe the fresh air of the mountains, but if you seek my authority you will remain in your dark valley of limitation. It is much easier for you to follow and worship blindly than to understand and so become truly free.

Until I was able to identify myself with the goal, which is the Beloved of all, which is the Source and the End of all, I did not want to say

LIFE IN FREEDOM

that I had found and in finding had become the Beloved. Till I was able to unite with the eternal I could not pass on the Truth to others; till I was certain of having found the lasting goal I did not want to say that I was the Teacher. Now that I have found, now that I have established the Beloved within myself, now that the Beloved is myself I would give you of the Truth—not that it should be received with authority but with understanding. It does not matter whether you accept or reject it. When a flower opens and gives its scent it does not heed if the passer-by does not delight in its fragrance.

I have painted my picture on the canvas and I want you to examine it critically, not blindly. I want you to create because of that picture a new picture for yourself. I want you to fall in love with the picture, not with the painter, to fall in love with the Truth and not with him who brings the Truth. Fall in love with yourself and then you will fall in love with every one.

In order to attain liberation it is not necessary to join any organization, any religion, because they are binding, they are limiting, they hold you to a particular form of worship and belief. If you long for freedom you will fight, as I have fought, against authority of any kind, for authority is the antithesis of spirituality. If I were to use authority to-day and you accepted my authority, it would not make you free, you would be merely following the freedom of another. In following the freedom of another, you are binding yourself more strongly to the wheel of limitation. Do not allow your mind or your heart to be bound by anything or by any one. If you do, you will establish another religion, another temple. While destroying one set of beliefs you will establish another set of beliefs. I am fighting against all traditions that bind, all worship that narrows, all following that corrupts the heart. If you would find that freedom to which I would point the way, you will begin, as I began, by being discontented, by being in revolt, in inner dissent with everything about you. You frequently use the phrase, "We will obey our leaders." Who are your leaders? I never want to be a leader. I never want to have authority. I want you to become your own leaders.

LIFE IN FREEDOM

Life is simple and magnificent, lovely and divine, but you want all the beauty and the freshness of the dawn and of the still night to be caught and held in a narrow circle so that you can worship it. Go down to the sea-beach of an evening when the fresh breezes are blowing and all the blades of grass are in motion and the particles of sand are flying about and the trees are waving their branches, and the waves of the sea are breaking over each other. You want to gather and bind all that beauty into a narrow temple. You need have no beliefs in order to live nobly. And yet you say, "I must worship Gods, I must perform rites, I must go to shrines, I must follow this and do that." It is an eternal *must*. That way of living is not living at all.

Whatever you do, do not create another temple around me. I shall not be held within it. I want to be your companion with the freshness of the breeze. I want to free you from your own limitations, to encourage within you individual creation, individual perfection, individual uniqueness. The self can only be purified and truly transcended when it has developed its own individual uniqueness to perfection; not when it is held in limitations, bound by tradi-

THE SEARCH

tions, by forms, and by all the unnecessary paraphernalia which you think essential to your well-being.

I remember a story written by a Norwegian—the hero of that story in search for freedom and happiness joins one religion after another and worships one God after another, performs one ceremony after another, and still he cannot find what he seeks. At length he becomes a Buddhist and drops his physical body and enters Nirvana. He enters the Nirvana of the books and there he sees all the Gods of all the religions seated and conversing with each other. They offer him a vacant seat. This hero appears as a flame, but this flame does not want to be caught and while all the Gods try to catch hold of him he disappears. The Gods cannot follow him because even Gods themselves are bound.

Do not be bound by me or by any one. Happiness is within yourself.

I set out to find for myself the purpose of life and I found it, without the authority of another. I have entered that sea of liberation and happiness in which there is no limitation or negation because it is the fulfillment of life.

LIFE IN FREEDOM

Because after my long journey towards attainment and perfection I have attained that perfection and established it in my heart, and because my mind is tranquil and eternally liberated as the flame, I would give of that understanding to all.

STAND IN YOUR OWN STRENGTH

STAND IN YOUR OWN STRENGTH

EVERY one in the world is concerned with the search for that Truth which will satisfy him eternally, but in that search each one contends against another; and hence there is confusion, struggle and pain. They lack the certainty of purpose which will determine their course through life and so rely on another for their comfort, well-being, and understanding.

Because they admit that they are weak, because they maintain that they cannot stand without the support of another, they have been given crutches that will support them momentarily, instead of developing their own strength to go forward in search of the pure waters of Truth.

If you would find that Truth you must put aside all those things upon which you have leaned for support and look within for that everlasting spring. It cannot be brought to you through any outward channel.

In search of the Truth that shall sustain, uphold, and guide you, you have looked outwards and sought for it objectively, and thus have been lost in the shadows of manifestation. To find that spring of Truth you must look within, you must purify your heart and mind.

You say to me, "You are different; you have attained, and because you have attained, these comforts are unnecessary for *you*." No, friend, because you desire to attain, these things are unnecessary for *you*. Because I have leaned on crutches to support me, I know the uselessness of crutches. When you have passed along a dangerous narrow path, and you have often slipped, and had to climb again, surely you would say to your fellow travelers, "Beware of these things, do not walk on the edge, walk rather in the middle, keeping your balance, and do not be led away, so that you fall over the precipice."

Because I know that your comforts only weaken you, I tell you to throw them away. Because I have been entangled in complexities, because I have been held in bondage, I urge you to escape into freedom. Because I have found a simple and direct path, I would tell you of it. If I had relied for my happiness on others, if I had been caught up in grandiloquent phrases, or in the worship of images, or persons, in the shadows of temples, I should not have found that Truth which I sought. Not in the worship of externals do you find the spring of Truth, but in the adoration of Truth itself.

Because you imagine that without all these complications of beliefs and systematized thoughts which are called religions, you cannot find Truth, that very thought is preventing you from finding it. If you would climb to a great height, if you would go far, you do not carry on your shoulders great burdens. In like manner, if you would attain liberation you do not cling to the burdens which you have accumulated throughout the ages. You must put aside those things which you have gained and reach out for further understanding.

In search of the waters that shall quench your thirst, if you are wise, you will not act in haste. Through haste you find nothing. By patient understanding, by careful watching that you may not be caught up in things that are trivial, non-essential, you find that which you seek. It is difficult for you to realize that your own understanding dwells within, that your happiness lies within yourself, because you have been accustomed to look to objective things for your understanding and your Truth.

LIFE IN FREEDOM

Invite doubt; for doubt is as a precious ointment: though it burns, it shall heal greatly—and by inviting doubt, by putting aside those things which you have understood, by transcending your acquirements, your understanding, you will find the Truth.

THE HIDDEN WELL

IN MEMORIAM

THE HIDDEN WELL

WHEN the fountain is sealed and the spring is shut up, to open that fountain and release that spring you must dig deep, and thereby disturb the earth. In like manner and for the same purpose there must be disturbance within you if you would find Truth. As the waters are hidden in the dry lands, so is Truth hidden in your heart. I would dig in each of you a well that shall nourish and sustain you, but to dig deep you must uproot greatly, to have great depth of water you must delve deeply into the earth. The process of digging creates discontentment and revolt, and the destruction of useless things. Love Truth for its own beauty, do right because you yourself desire to do it, and develop the inward perception of true understanding. If you follow without understanding, you will betray the Truth, and because I hold the Truth with such care, with such gratitude for its loveliness, I want you not to betray it. For this reason I am creating revolt within you, I am digging deep to discover the waters that shall nourish you, the Truth that shall give you tranquillity; the Truth that shall give you ecstasy of purpose in this world of confusion. If you merely repeat after me new phrases instead of the old, that repetition will not show the way to Truth. There must be a vital change in the mind and in the heart before that inward perception of Truth which is the true understanding of life, can be developed. Do not settle down more comfortably in your already comfortable attitude of mind, for satisfaction and contentment do not lead to the Truth, neither do they bring happiness. Become a genius by developing your own individual uniqueness. The genius of one man can never be complete; the genius which is the outcome of the individual uniqueness of many, which all have helped to produce, will alone be perfect. If you would create greatly, if you would have that creation last eternally, you must develop your own individual uniqueness, your own perfection, with the understanding of the Truth, and not imitate the perfection of another.

BE IN LOVE WITH LIFE

BE IN LOVE WITH LIFE

DURING the time of winter, every tree looks forward to the warm airs of the spring, but when that spring comes, if there is no life in the tree it will not put forth green foliage, flowers and fruit. I am telling you of that life which is in all things, and in keeping that life pure, strong and vital, you will find happiness—not in limiting that life and placing it in bondage. Every one in the world is more concerned with the branches and leaves of the tree than with the sap which gives vitality to the whole tree. I am concerned with the life of the tree, and not with the branch, the leaf, the flower and the fruit; because I hold that as long as the life in the tree is healthy, its expression is bound to be beautiful. In the same way if the life in you is strong, vital and pure, you will attain to that Truth which is unlimited and cannot be conditioned. If you seek to condition it, it is betrayed.

You are all concerned with the appearance of the tree, with the pruning of its branches, with the examination of its leaves, you are intoxicated with its perfume and you are not pleased when you are called back to the consideration of that which produces your tree, with its perfume, its leaves and its branches. As there is no life in a dead branch, it is broken by the winter winds and drops away. Such will be the man who does not put life before all lesser things, who does not release life from its bondage, from the trivialities that have been imposed upon it. In order to free life you must be in love with life. You would much rather adore an image than worship life itself.

Do not put aside what I am saying with a shrug of your shoulders, but listen diligently, and you will understand greatly. If you are prejudiced, if you are determined to twist life to suit your particular beliefs, your particular branch of the expression of life, then you will not find the Truth.

In order to release that spring which will develop into a torrent and hence carry you to the attainment of liberation which is Truth, which is the fulfillment of life, you must discover what is essential for your understanding, and set aside all those things which are of secondary importance.

BE IN LOVE WITH LIFE

You will be unhappy; you will struggle; you will have to go through disappointments, anxieties, great agonies, if you place the unessential before the essential. That is what you are all doing, because to you life and the freedom of life, is not important. When you are in love with life you will invite sorrow, doubt, every experience, in order that you may conquer every experience, that you may break the bondages which you have placed on life.

To find the Truth, you must give up the worship of the image and fall in love with life. Then you will become immortal. The fear of death disappears in him who is in love with life and who sees that life in the eyes of his neighbor. Be in love with life, and loyal to life and not to persons, because the worship of personalities does not lead you to Truth. Truth does not belong to any individual, Truth does not belong to any religion, Truth cannot be found in the dark sanctuary of temples, nor in the well-lit halls of organized societies, neither can it be found in books, nor in ceremonies. I would bring you to the understanding of Truth, but you would much rather have me repeat what you have heard a hundred times. You would much rather that I put you to sleep, lull you in comfort, than awaken in you the desire to shatter all things, to discover life.

If you would discover the cause for all the beauty of the world, for all the dancing shadows, do not be caught up in the illusion of the expressions of life, but rather seek for that Truth which is life itself by being in love with life.

TIME

TIME

FOR those who have discovered Truth and attained the fulfillment of life—which is happiness and liberation—time and the complications of time have ceased. But those who are still bound to the yoke of experience are limited by the past, present and future.

You who would discover the Truth which is absolute and infinite, must realize that you are the product of the past, and the outcome of your own creation. You are bringing forth out of yourself that which you have sown in the past. And as man is the product of the past, so by his actions of to-day he can control the future. To-morrow depends upon to-day, and therefore to-day determines to-morrow. By controlling the future you become the master of the future. You bring the future to the present.

Every one throughout the world is bound by the traditions, the fears, the shame, the beliefs, the morality, of the past. If you are constantly looking backwards, you will never discover

Truth. The discovery of eternal Truth lies always ahead of you. If you truly understand this, you will not cling to the past. You will not be always conditioned by the thoughts, the actions, the feelings, the ethics of the past, because therein is stagnation and the bondage of life. Cut away the bondage of the past as a woodman cuts his way through a dark forest to find the open spaces and fresh breezes. For the past always binds, however glorious, however well seasoned, however fruitful it may have been, and the man who would be free must look eternally forward.

If you would walk, and build, and create in the shelter of eternity, you must not bring the past into conflict with the present, but must invite the future and thereby bring that future into conflict with the present.

Because your mind and heart are bound by traditions and beliefs, by the sacred books of the past, by the dark shadows of temples and remembered gods, you do not understand either the present or the future. Time, as man understands it, is dividing you from your goal. Therefore, to bring time to naught, you must so live now that you are the master of the future, so that the future becomes the present.

TIME

People love to think of themselves as being glorified in the future, or resting on the laurels of what they have been in the past. What a comforting idea! The belief in your greatness in some distant future will not help you to deal with life in the present, when you are struggling, when there is confusion in your mind and heart.

Not in the distant future did I want to be great, but I desired to be happy in the present, I wanted to be free in the present, I wanted to be beyond all the limitations of time. So I invited the future into the present, and hence I have conquered the future.

Do not live in the future, nor in the dead things of yesterday, but live rather in the immediate now, with the understanding that you are a product of the past, and that by your actions of to-day you can control to-morrow and so become the master of time, the master of evolution, and hence the master of perfection.

Then you will live with greater intensity, then every second will count and every moment be of value. But you are frightened of such a present. You would much rather be conditioned by the past, because you have a dread of

LIFE IN FREEDOM

the future. But the future is not fearsome to those who walk in the way of understanding. If you would attain to the fulfillment of life, you must invite the future to the present and thereby create a conflict within yourself. Through contentment you do not find happiness, but a state of stagnation. If you would know true happiness there must first be that inward conflict, which will bring forth in you the flower of life.

Put aside the past with all its glories, beautiful and terrible, all its traditions, wide and yet so conditioned, all its moralities that strangle life, and look into your own heart and mind to discover what lies before you in the future. For as you are the product of the past, and as you can control the future, so the future becomes the present and you live in that present.

FORMLESS CREATION

FORMLESS CREATION

FROM these Camps you will go away to all parts of the world carrying with you that which you have understood, and carrying with you, alas, also that which you have not understood. If that which you have not understood be the stronger, because of its strength, it will pervert that which you have understood. I would give you the flower of understanding which shall know no decay, so that you may keep it ever with you.

Truth is like a flame without definite form, it varies from moment to moment. No man can describe it, but by the light of Truth alone you must walk, if you would keep that flower of understanding with you always.

Because you will go away with phrases, with words, with half ideas, the full beauty of manifestation will escape you. I have heard people say, "I must give up music. I must no longer admire painting. I must no longer enjoy the shade of a tree and the glory of sunset; nor the reflection of the swallow on a still evening on the face of the waters." If that is what you understand when I say that life is more important than its expressions, you will destroy the beauty of the expression, and then you will have to create that beauty again. Do you think that there is so much beauty around us in expression, in manifestation, only to be destroyed, to be put aside and not to be admired?

As the water is necessary for the beauty of the lotus, and as the lotus makes the waters beautiful, so, when the expression of life is destroyed, when it is made hideous and horrible to behold, then life itself, which is in each one, becomes perverted, mutilated and ugly. So, friend, do not cease to admire beauty. Do not hold back the laughter that awakens in your heart when you see a dancing leaf. Do not thwart the expressions of life by misunderstanding the purpose of life. To bring that expression to perfection, to its fulfillment, life must be free, life must not be bound by traditions, by your stagnating moralities and beliefs. The expressions of life will then be naturally beautiful.

There have been many thousand people at these Camps, and what could they not do in the world if they all understood? They could

FORMLESS CREATION

change the face of the world to-morrow. Its expression would become different because new life had been brought to it.

That is what I long to do. That is the only desire that burns in my heart. Because I see sadness and corruption, pain and suffering, passing ecstasies and passing fantasies, I would awaken life and bring it to its perfect fulfillment. You who are going away must realize your responsibility. Truth is not to be played with, nor to be corrupted by misunderstanding, but to be developed with full understanding of the purpose of life. If you have caught a glimpse of Truth, if you are walking on the path of understanding, you can change the thought and feeling of the world; but before you can change the world, you must change your own heart and mind. For this reason you have gathered together, for this reason you have been shaken to the very foundation—as I hope—of your structure. You have come to discover, in the light of the Truth, that which is lasting, which shall stand against the storm, and distinguish it from that which is unimportant, trivial and to be set aside.

For that reason I have urged you to invite doubt, and to examine with understanding all that you have gathered through the ages. Adversity is as a furnace through which every one must pass. Great struggles, great sorrows and great ecstasies unfold the Truth in its sublimity, in its simplicity. To welcome adversity—not thrust upon you by another—you must invite doubt. If doubt unconsciously insinuates itself into your heart, it will not purify it. You can only purify it by deliberately inviting doubt.

Those who would attain greatly, who would understand truly must invite the future, and let that future come into conflict with the fruit of the past, which is the present. But you do not want to do that. All your questions, all your thoughts and feelings have been about the past. You have judged everything that I have put before you by the past; but, friend, Truth is neither bound by the past nor the present nor the future. To understand Truth, you must put aside all things that you have accumulated and not cling with fear to the past, however beautiful it may be. If the past seems so fruitful to you, if the past in its decay is so dear to you, if the past holds such sway over you, why are you here? You are here because you are faced with the future. To understand the future you must put aside the past and take the future to your heart and mind, and cling to it desperately as a drowning man desires air. Not merely to dwell in some distant future, but to bring that future into the immediate present is the glory of man. I tell you, friend, One greater than your books, your rites, your religions and your beliefs, is here, and if you would learn to understand the Truth, you must put aside the past, however comfortable, however pleasing, however delightful it may have been, and welcome the future. If you worship and cling to the past, you will be like the dead stumps of yesterday; no waters can revive their green shoots.

As you have to build greatly, you must bring that future Truth and life in its fulfillment to the present. To create greatly, to create lastingly, you must understand, and so I say, "Do not follow, do not obey, do not be loyal to any person except to yourself, and then you will be loyal to every passer-by."

Do not repeat after me words that you do not understand. Do not merely put on a mask of my ideas, for it will be an illusion and you will thereby deceive yourself.

I would build in your heart and mind that Truth which is of no form and hence eternal.

LIFE IN FREEDOM

I would change your heart and mind in the shadow of eternity. When you change and build on the love of life and its understanding, what you build will be everlasting. I do not want to concern myself with the molding of a door, which is but an expression of life. You can always change the expression of life, but if you would build eternally in the light of the Truth, you must ever give love to life, with new ideas and understanding to nourish it. The only eternal creation is that which is without form, with life itself and not with the expressions of life. You want me to create your expressions, to lay down disciplines for you to follow; you want me, who am the Life, to deal with the moldings of the door. Because I do not concern myself with the expressions and manifestations of life, you are not satisfied. You want me to deal with the transitory instead of with the eternal.

Friend, I want to lay the foundation of Truth in your mind and heart. That is the work of life and therefore of the eternal. You have not so far been concerned with that foundation, you have not taken to heart and pondered over that Truth, you have all the time occupied yourself with the past, with small misunderstandings, with the corruption from obedience, with petty loyalties to individuals, with the adoration of passing mediators and *gurus*. Is it not better to seek the Life eternal that shall nourish you always, than to seek shelters that vary from moment to moment, inviting you to their decay and stagnation?

Friend, believe me, I am saying all this out of the fullness of my heart. Because I am in love with that life which is in every one, I would free that life; but you do not want that, you want the passing love, the fleeting comfort and the balm that shall heal your momentary pain. You desire what you perceive, but if your perception is limited and conditioned, your desire will be the cause of your sorrow. But if your perception has no limitation, if it is beyond all beliefs and traditions, then your desire will have no limitations, it will be life itself. You are not in love with life; you are in love with the past, and life is not concerned with the past. Life, like the swift running waters, is always going forward and is never still and stagnant.

Because One greater than all these is with you, I hold it dear and precious that you should understand in the fullness of your heart and mind, and so create the light which shall be your guide, which is not the light of another but your own. Go away with the mirror of Truth which shall reflect your life, with the love that is detached, and with the understanding of the Truth.

THE DISSOLUTION OF THE ORDER OF THE STAR

A STATEMENT BY

J. KRISHNAMURTI

January 11, 1911 Benares

August 3, 1929 Ommen

THE BOOK TREE
San Diego, California

For the benefit of those who know nothing of the Order of the Star and for whom its dissolution, therefore, can have no meaning, we give here a brief explanation.

The Order of the Star in the East was founded in Benares, India, in the year 1911, to proclaim the coming of a World-Teacher and to prepare the world for that event. J. Krishnamurti was placed at the head of that Order by those who recognised the potential Teacher in him.

In 1927 the name of the Order was changed to "Order of the Star", as its members realised that the days of expectation were over and Krishnamurti was for them the Teacher.

In 1929 Krishnamurti, by his own act, dissolves the Order, and his reasons for this action are contained in this pronouncement.

OMMEN CAMP, AUGUST 3, 1929

THE DISSOLUTION OF THE ORDER OF THE STAR
A STATEMENT BY J. KRISHNAMURTI

We are going to discuss this morning the dissolution of the Order of the Star. Many people will be delighted, and others will be rather sad. It is a question neither for rejoicing nor for sadness, because it is inevitable, as I am going to explain.

You may remember the story of how the devil and a friend of his were walking down the street, when they saw ahead of them a man stoop down and pick up something from the ground, look at it, and put it away in his pocket. The friend said to the devil, "What did that man pick up?" "He picked up a piece of Truth," said the devil. "That is a very bad business for you, then," said his friend. "Oh, not at all," the devil replied, "I am going to let him organise it."

I maintain that Truth is a pathless land, and you cannot approach it by any path whatsoever, by any religion, by any sect. That is my point of view, and I adhere to that absolutely and unconditionally. Truth, being limitless, unconditioned, unapproachable by any path whatsoever, cannot be organised; nor should any organisation be formed to lead or to coerce people along any particular path. If you first understand that, then you will see how impossible it is to organise a belief. A belief is purely an individual matter, and you cannot and must not organise it. If you do, it becomes dead, crystallised; it becomes a creed, a sect, a religion, to be imposed on others. This is what everyone throughout the world is attempting to do. Truth is narrowed down and made a plaything for those who are weak, for those who are only momentarily discontented. Truth cannot be brought down, rather the individual must make the effort to ascend to it. You cannot bring the mountain-top to the valley. If you would attain to the mountain-top you must pass through the valley, climb the steeps, unafraid of the dangerous precipices. You must climb towards the Truth, it cannot be "stepped down" or organised for you. Interest in ideas is mainly sustained by organisations, but organisations only awaken interest from without. Interest, which is not born out of love of Truth for its own sake, but aroused by an organisation, is of no value. The organisation becomes a framework into which its members can conveniently fit. They no longer strive after Truth or the mountain-top, but rather carve for themselves a convenient niche in which they put themselves or let the organisation place them and consider that the organisation will thereby lead them to Truth.

So that is the first reason, from my point of view, why the Order of the Star should be dissolved. In spite of this, you will probably form other Orders, you will continue to belong to other organisations searching for Truth. I do not want to belong to any organisation of a spiritual kind, please understand this. I would make use of an organisation which would take me to London, for example; this is quite a different kind of organisation, merely mechanical, like the post or the telegraph. I would use a motor car or a steamship to travel, these are only physical mechanisms which have nothing whatever to do with spirituality. Again, I maintain that no organisation can lead man to spirituality.

If an organisation be created for this purpose, it becomes a crutch, a weakness, a bondage, and must cripple the individual, and prevent him from growing, from establishing his uniqueness, which lies in the discovery for himself of that absolute, unconditioned Truth. So that is another reason why I have decided, as I happen to be the Head of the Order, to dissolve it. No one has persuaded me to this decision.

This is no magnificent deed, because I do not want followers, *and I mean this*. The moment you follow someone you cease to follow Truth. I am not concerned whether you pay attention to what I say or not. I want to do a certain thing in the world and I am going to do it with unwavering concentration. I am concerning myself with only one essential thing; to set man free. I desire to free him from all cages, from all fears, and not to found religions, new sects, nor to establish new theories and new philosophies. Then you will naturally ask me why I go the world over, continually speaking. I will tell you for what reason I do this: not because I desire a following, not because I desire a special group of special disciples. (How men love to be different from their fellow-men, however ridiculous, absurd and trivial their distinctions may be! I do not want to encourage that absurdity.) I have no disciples, no apostles, either on earth or in the realm of spirituality.

Nor is it the lure of money, nor the desire to live a comfortable life, which attracts me. If I wanted to lead a comfortable life I would not come to a Camp or live in a damp country! I am speaking frankly because I want this settled once and for all. I do not want these childish discussions year after year.

One newspaper reporter, who interviewed me, considered it a magnificent act to dissolve an organisation in which there were thousands and thousands of members. To him it was a great act because, he said: "What will you do afterwards, how will you live? You will have no following, people will no longer listen to you." If there are only five people who will listen, who will *live*, who have their faces turned towards eternity, it will be sufficient. Of what use is it to have thousands who do not understand, who are fully embalmed in prejudice, who do not want the new, but would rather translate the new to suit their own sterile, stagnant selves? If I speak strongly, please do not misunderstand me, it is not through lack of compassion. If you go to a surgeon for an operation, is it not kindness on his part to operate even if he cause you pain? So, in like manner, if I speak straightly, it is not through lack of real affection — on the contrary.

As I have said, I have only one purpose: to make man free, to urge him towards freedom, to help him to break away from all limitations, for that alone will give him eternal happiness, will give him the unconditioned realisation of the self.

Because I am free, unconditioned, whole, not the part, not the relative, but the whole Truth that is eternal, I desire those, who seek to understand me, to be free, not to follow me, not to make out of me a cage which will become a religion, a sect. Rather should they be free from all fears — from the fear of religion, from the fear of salvation, from the fear of spirituality, from the fear of love, from the fear of death, from the fear of life itself. As an artist paints a picture because he takes delight in that painting, because it is his self-expression, his glory, his well-being, so I do this and not because I want any thing from anyone.

You are accustomed to authority, or to the atmosphere of authority, which you think will lead you to spirituality. You think and hope that another can, by his extraordinary powers — a miracle — transport you to this realm of eternal freedom which is Happiness. Your whole outlook on life is based on that authority.

You have listened to me for three years now, without any change taking place except in the few. Now analyse what I am saying, be critical, so that you may understand thoroughly, fundamentally. When you look for an authority to lead you to spirituality, you are bound automatically to build an organisation around that authority. By the very creation of that organisation, which, you think, will help this authority to lead you to spirituality, you are held in a cage.

If I talk frankly, please remember that I do so, not out of harshness, not out of cruelty, not out of the enthusiasm of my purpose, but because I want you to understand what I am saying. That is the reason why you are here, and it would be a waste of time if I did not explain clearly, decisively, my point of view.

For eighteen years you have been preparing for this event, for the Coming of the World-Teacher.

For eighteen years you have organised, you have looked for someone who would give a new delight to your hearts and minds, who would transform your whole life, who would give you a new understanding; for someone who would raise you to a new plane of life, who would give you a new encouragement, who would set you free — and now look what is happening! Consider, reason with yourselves, and discover in what way that belief has made you different — not with the superficial difference of the wearing of a badge, which is trivial, absurd. In what manner has such a belief swept away all the unessential things of life? That is the only way to judge: in what way are you freer, greater, more dangerous to every Society which is based on the false and the unessential? In what way have the members of this organisation of the Star become different?

As I said, you have been preparing for eighteen years for me. I do not care if you believe that I am the World-Teacher or not. That is of very little importance. Since you belong to the organisation of the Order of the Star, you have given your sympathy, your energy, acknowledging that Krishnamurti is the World-Teacher — partially or wholly: wholly for those who are really seeking, only partially for those who are satisfied with their own half-truths.

You have been preparing for eighteen years,

and look how many difficulties there are in the way of your understanding, how many complications, how many trivial things. Your prejudices, your fears, your authorities, your churches new and old — all these, I maintain, are a barrier to understanding. I cannot make myself clearer than this. I do not want you to agree with me, I do not want you to follow me, I want you to understand what I am saying.

This understanding is necessary because your belief has not transformed you but only complicated you, and because you are not willing to face things as they are. You want to have your own gods — new gods instead of the old, new religions instead of the old, new forms instead of the old — all equally valueless, all barriers, all limitations, all crutches. Instead of old spiritual distinctions you have new spiritual distinctions, instead of old worships you have new worships. You are all depending for your spirituality on someone else, for your happiness on someone else, for your enlightenment on someone else; and although you have been preparing for me for eighteen years, when I say all these things are unnecessary, when I say that you must put them all away and look within yourselves for the enlightenment, for the glory, for the purification, and for the incorruptibility of the self, not one of you is willing to do it. There may be a few, but very, very few.

So why have an organisation?

Why have false, hypocritical people following me, the embodiment of Truth? Please remember that I am not saying something harsh or unkind, but we have reached a situation when you must face things as they are. I said last year that I would not compromise. Very few listened to me then. This year I have made it absolutely clear. I do not know how many thousands throughout the world — members of the Order — have been preparing for me for eighteen years, and yet now they are not willing to listen unconditionally, wholly, to what I say.

So why have an organisation?

As I said before, my purpose is to make men unconditionally free, for I maintain that the only spirituality is the incorruptibility of the self which is eternal, is the harmony between reason and love. This is the absolute, unconditioned Truth which is Life itself. I want therefore to set man free, rejoicing as the bird in the clear sky, unburdened, independent, ecstatic in that freedom. And I, for whom you have been preparing for eighteen years, now say that you must be free of all these things, free from your complications, your entanglements. For this you need not have an organisation based on spiritual belief. Why have an organisation for five or ten people in the world who understand, who are struggling, who have put aside all trivial things? And for the weak people, there can be no organisation to help them to find the Truth, because Truth is in everyone; it is not far, it is not near; it is eternally there.

Organisations cannot make you free. No man from outside can make you free; nor can organised worship, nor the immolation of yourselves for a cause, make you free; nor can forming yourselves into an organisation, nor throwing yourselves into works, make you free. You use a typewriter to write letters, but you do not put it on an altar and worship it. But that is what you are doing when organisations become your chief concern. "How many members are there in it?" That is the first question I am asked by all newspaper reporters. "How many followers have you? By their number we shall judge whether what you say is true or false." I do not know how many there are. I am not concerned with that. As I said, if there were even one man who had been set free, that were enough.

Again, you have the idea that only certain people hold the key to the Kingdom of Happiness. No one holds it. No one has the authority to hold that key. That key is your own self, and in the development and the purification and in the incorruptibility of that self alone is the Kingdom of Eternity.

So you will see how absurd is the whole

structure that you have built, looking for external help, depending on others for your comfort, for your happiness, for your strength. These can only be found within yourselves.

So why have an organisation?

You are accustomed to being told how far you have advanced, what is your spiritual status. How childish! Who but yourself can tell you if you are beautiful or ugly within? Who but yourself can tell you if you are incorruptible? You are not serious in these things.

So why have an organisation?

But those who really desire to understand, who are looking to find that which is eternal, without beginning and without an end, will walk together with a greater intensity, will be a danger to everything that is unessential, to unrealities, to shadows. And they will concentrate, they will become the flame, because they understand. Such a body we must create, and that is my purpose. Because of that real understanding there will be true friendship. Because of that true friendship — which you do not seem to know — there will be real cooperation on the part of each one. And this not because of authority, not because of salvation, not because of immolation for a cause, but because you really understand, and hence are capable of living in the eternal. This is a greater thing than all pleasure, than all sacrifice.

So those are some of the reasons why, after careful consideration for two years, I have made this decision. It is not from a momentary impulse. I have not been persuaded to it by anyone — I am not persuaded in such things. For two years I have been thinking about this, slowly, carefully, patiently, and I have now decided to disband the Order, as I happen to be its Head. You can form other organisations and expect someone else. With that I am not concerned, nor with creating new cages, new decorations for those cages. My only concern is to set men absolutely, unconditionally free.

www.ingramcontent.com/pod-product-compliance
Lightning Source LLC
Chambersburg PA
CBHW060844050426
42453CB00008B/820